SCHIRMER'S LIBRARY
OF MUSICAL CLASSICS

Vol. 2140

16 NOCTURNES FOR PIANO

CONTENTS

ISBN 978-1-5400-3967-5

G. SCHIRMER, Inc.

DISTRIBUTED BY
HAL•LEONARD®
7777 W. BLUEMOUND RD. P.O. BOX 13819 MILWAUKEE, WI 53213

à Madame Camilla Pleyel

Nocturne in B-flat minor

Frédéric Chopin
Op. 9, No. 1

Larghetto (♩ = 116)

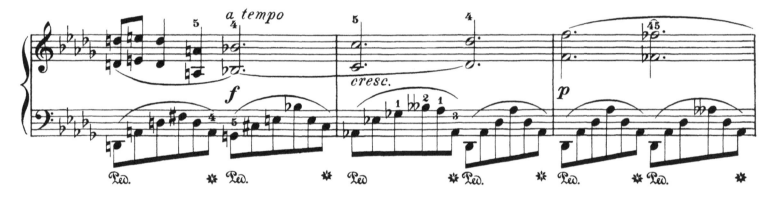

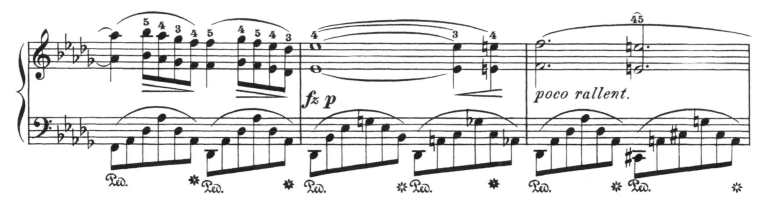

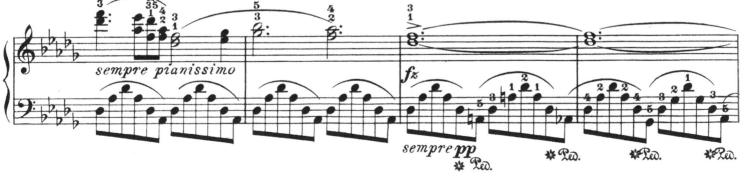

à Madame Camilla Pleyel

Nocturne in E-flat Major

Frédéric Chopin
Op. 9, No. 2

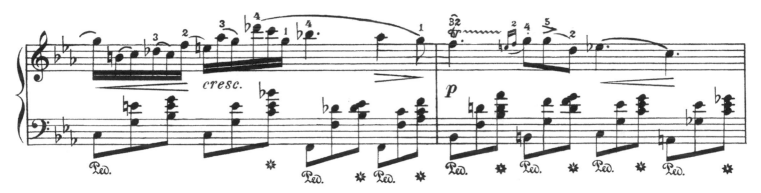

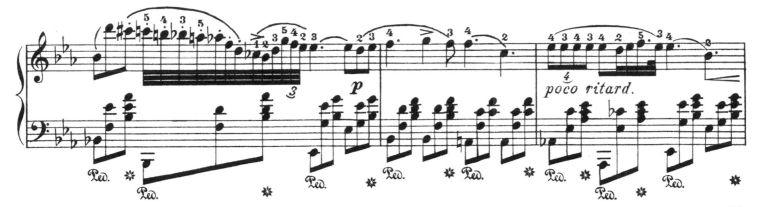

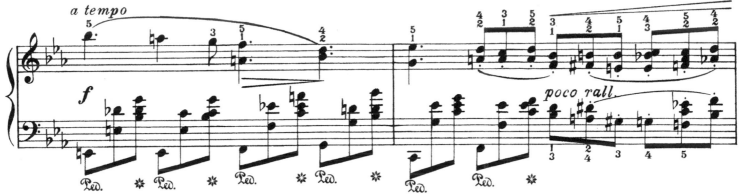

à Madame la Contesse d'Appony

Nocturne in C-sharp minor

Frédéric Chopin
Op. 27, No. 1

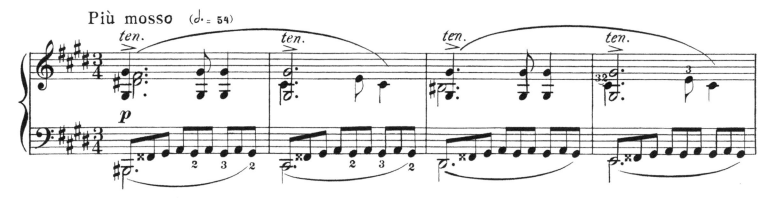

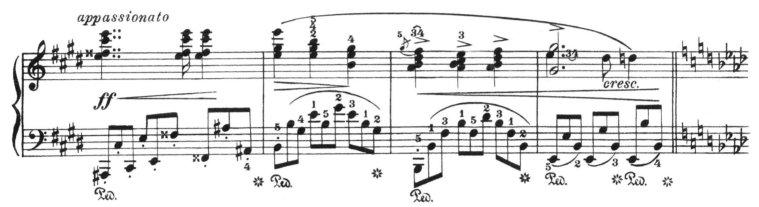

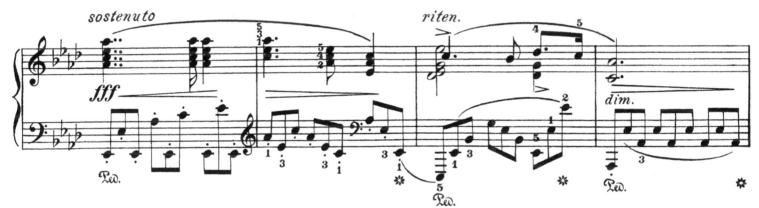

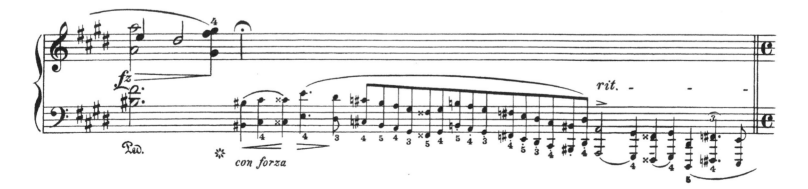

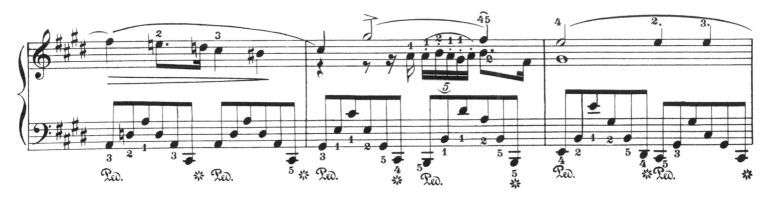

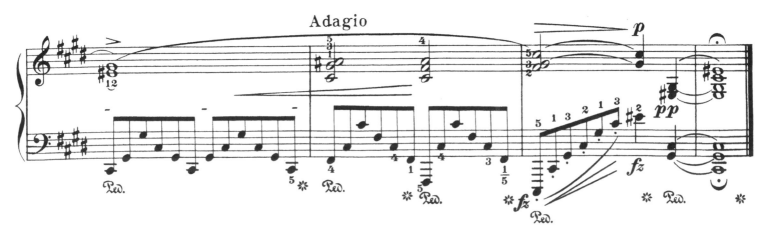

à Madame la Contesse d'Appony

Nocturne in D-flat Major

Frédéric Chopin
Op. 27, No. 2

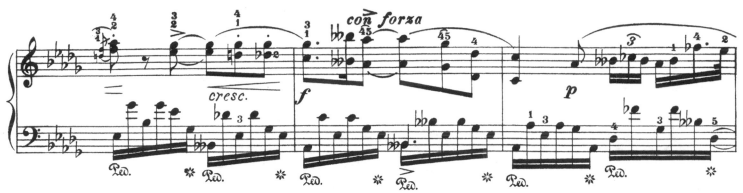

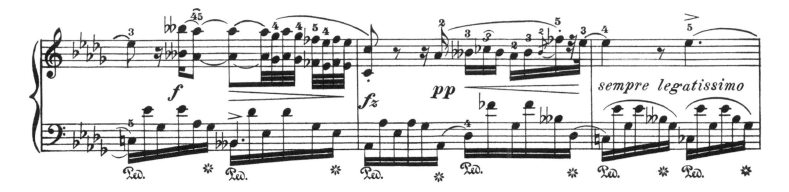

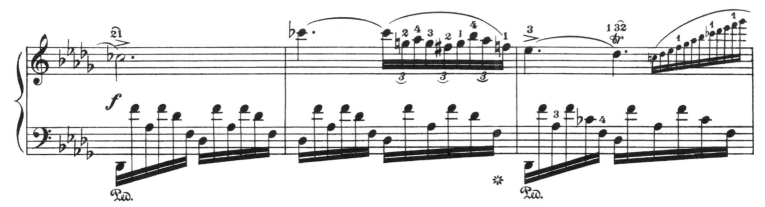

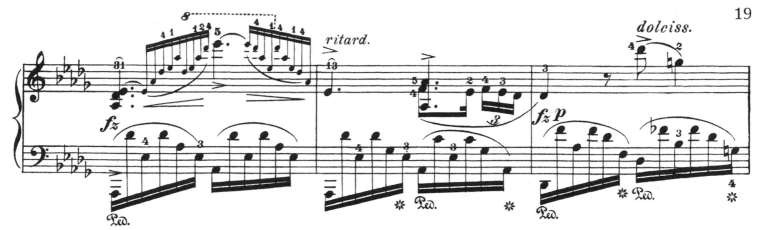

à Madame la Contesse d'Appony

Nocturne in C minor

Frédéric Chopin
Op. 48, No. 1

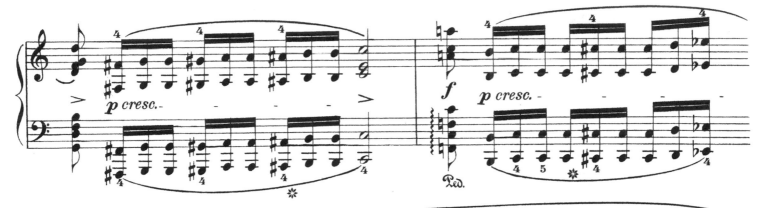

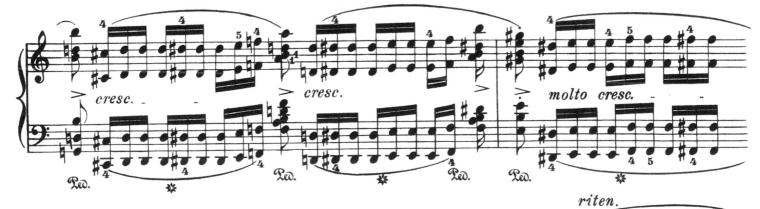

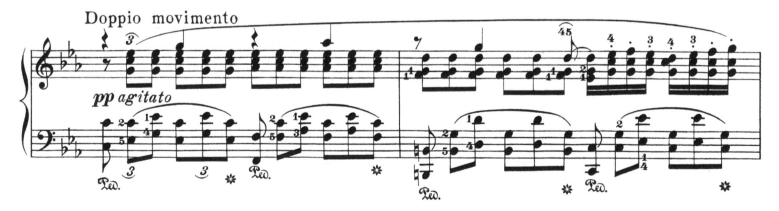

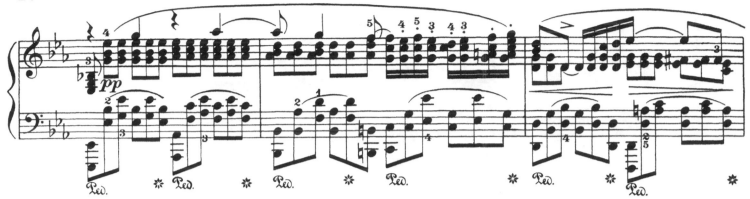

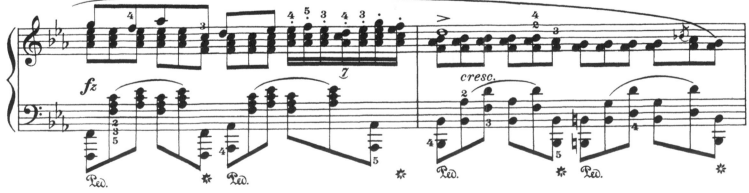

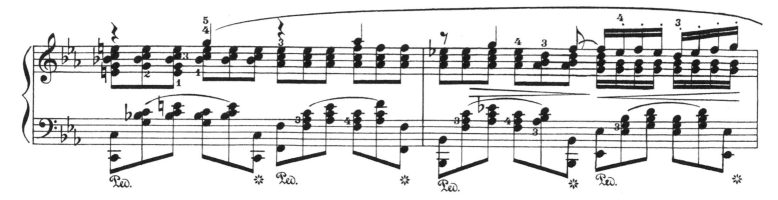

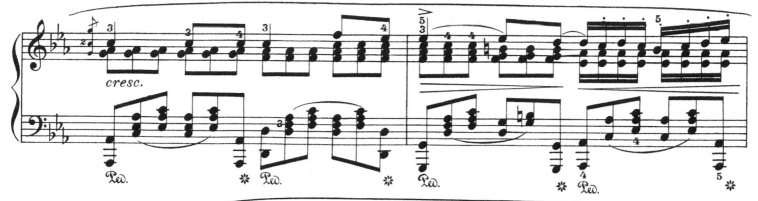

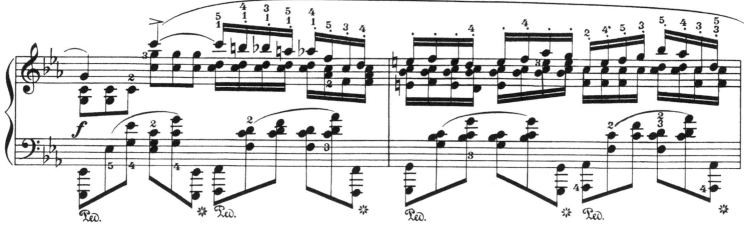

Nocturne

Claude Debussy

animando poco a poco

a tempo

più dim.

p

dolcissimo

p

ritenendo

Allegretto (♪=♪)

ppp *(In the style of a popular song)*

ancora a tempo

Nocturne No. 4 in E-flat Major

Gabriel Fauré
Op. 36

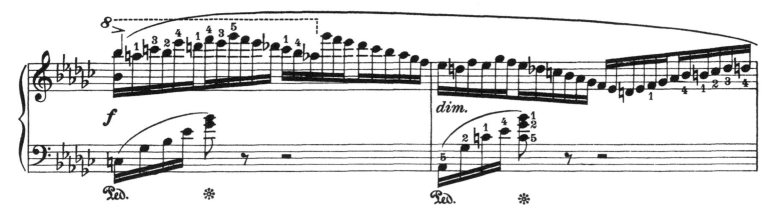

Notturno
from *Lyric Pieces*

Edvard Grieg
Op. 54, No. 4

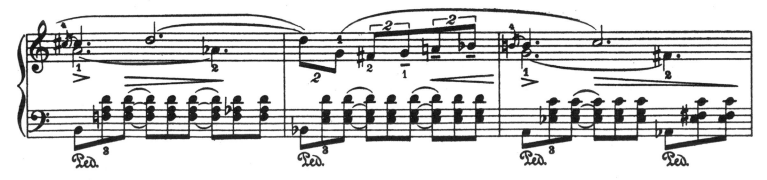

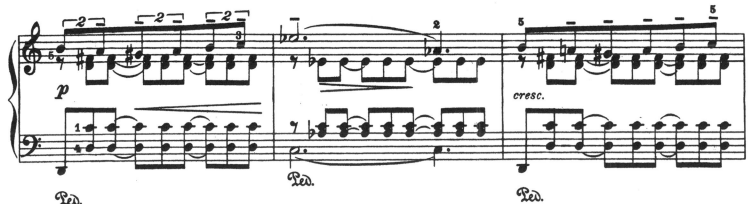

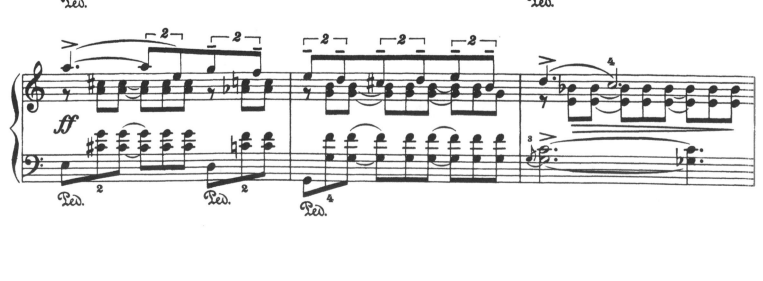

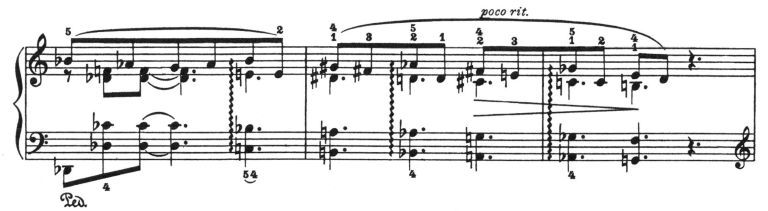

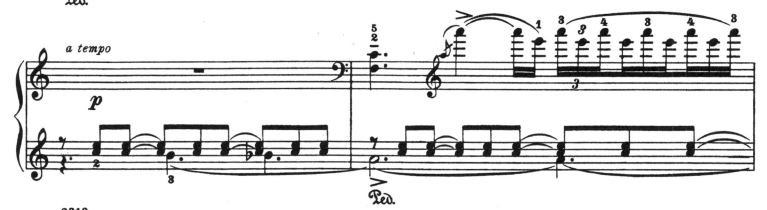

Liebesträum No. 1

from *Three Liebesträume: Three Notturnos*

Franz Liszt

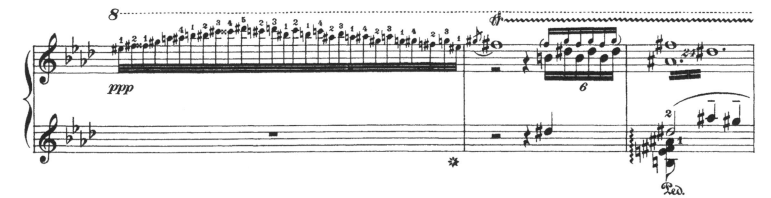

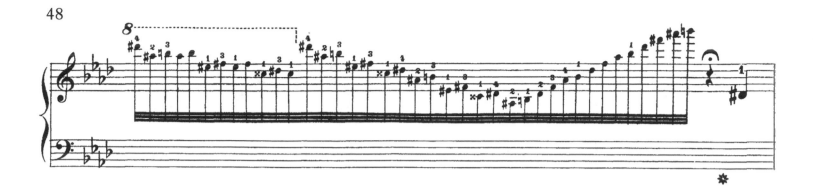

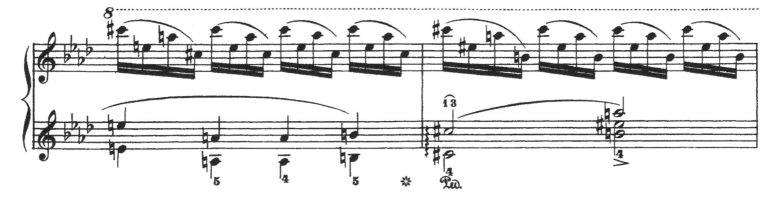

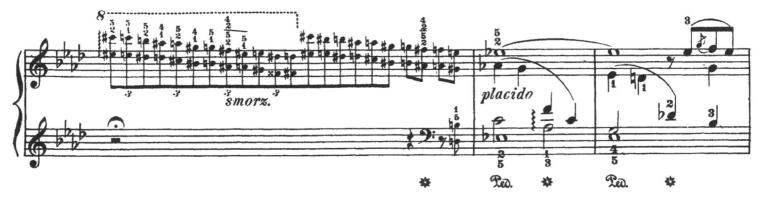

Liebesträum No. 2

from *Three Liebesträume: Three Notturnos*

Franz Liszt

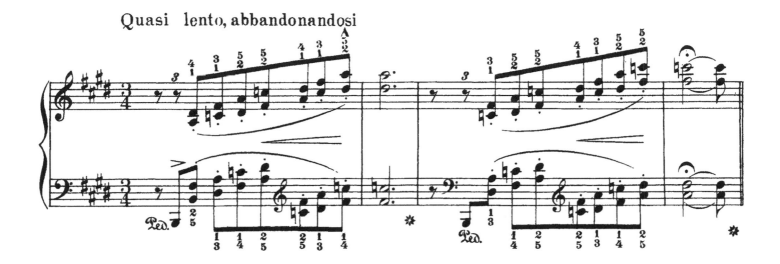

52

sempre marcato il canto
armonioso

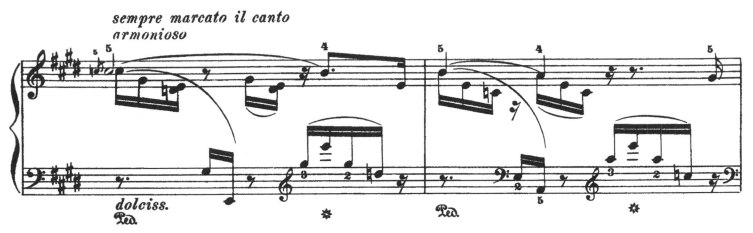

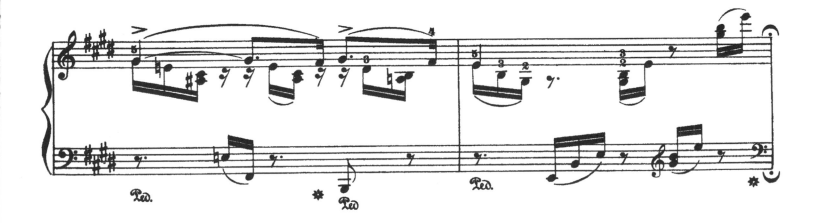

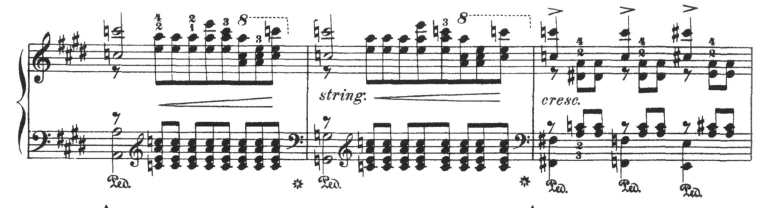

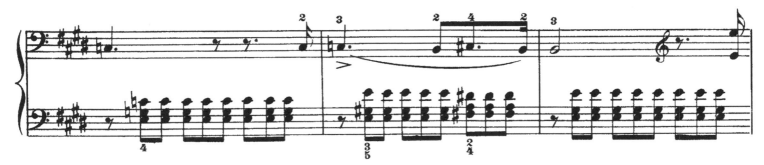

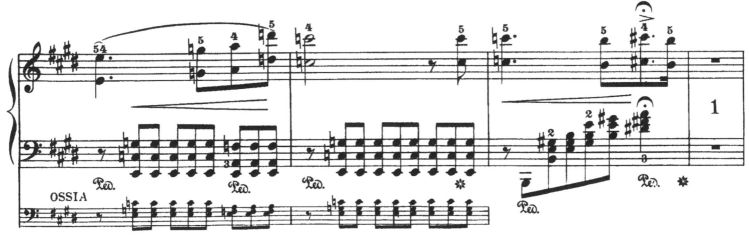

Liebestraum No. 3

from *Three Liebesträume: Three Notturnos*

Franz Liszt

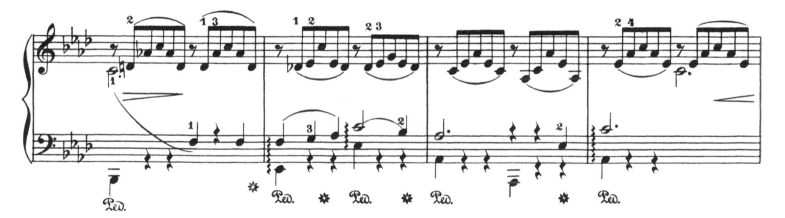

poco cresc. ed agitato

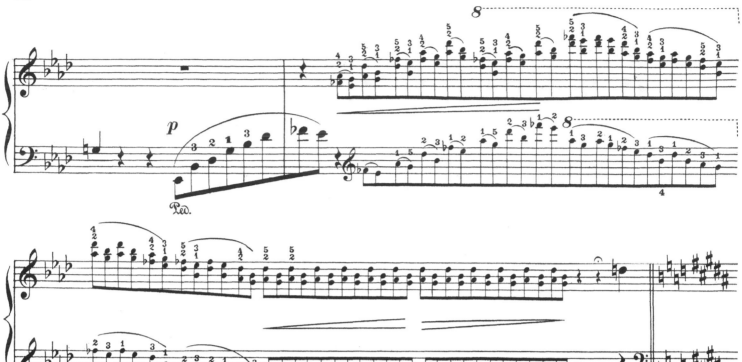

Più animato, con passione

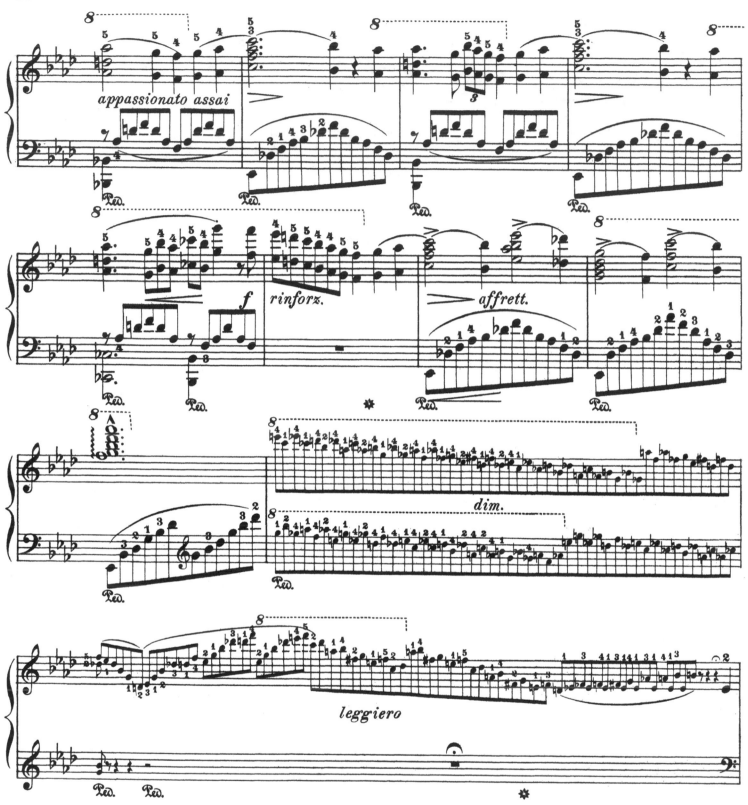

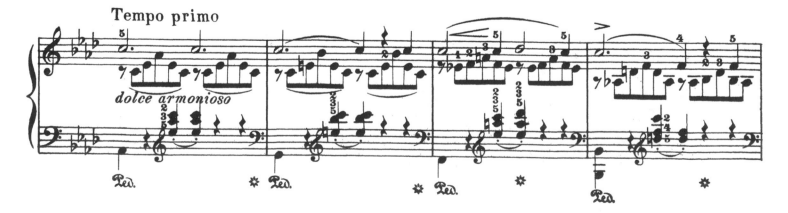

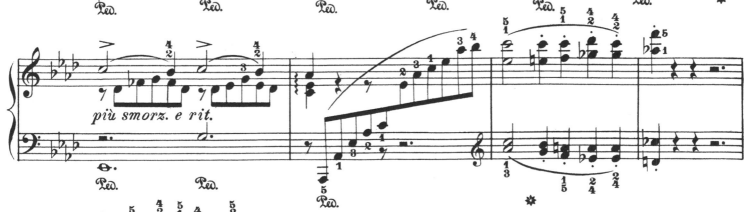

Nocturne in F Major

Pyotr Il'yich Tchaikovsky
Op. 10, No. 1

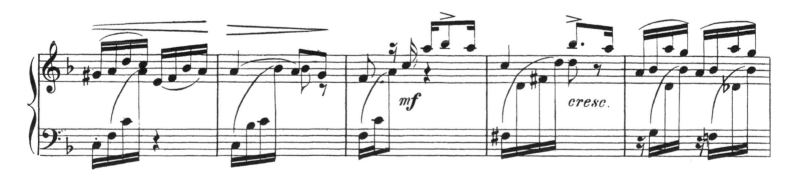

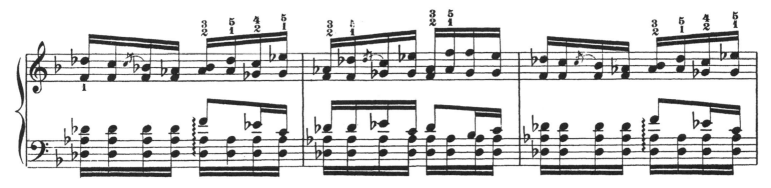

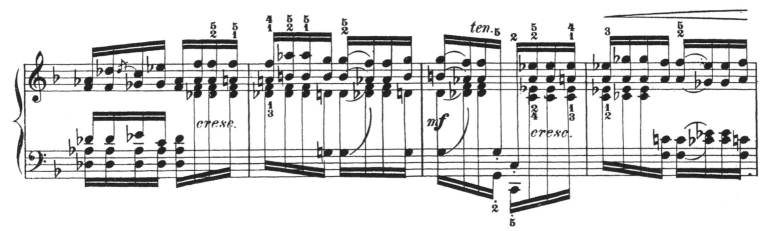

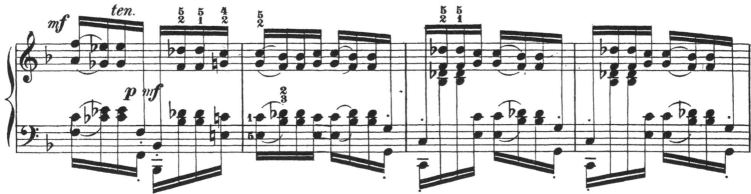

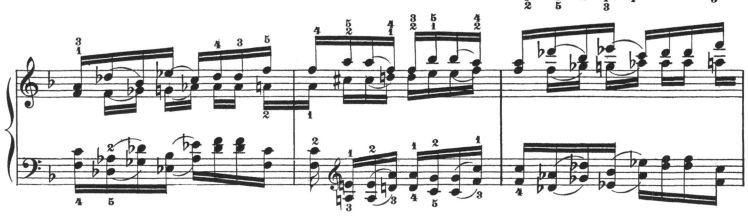

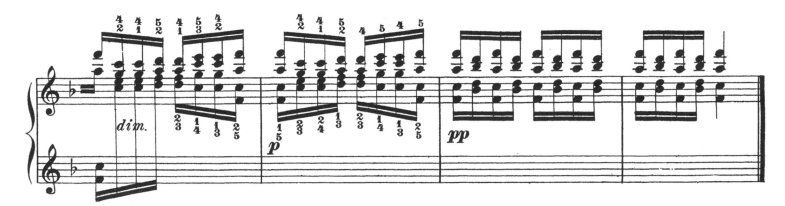

Nocturne No. 3 in A-flat Major

John Field

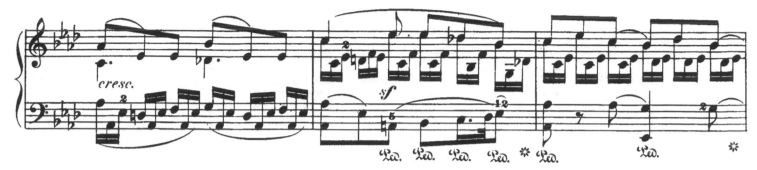

Nocturne No. 6 in F Major
Cradle Song

John Field

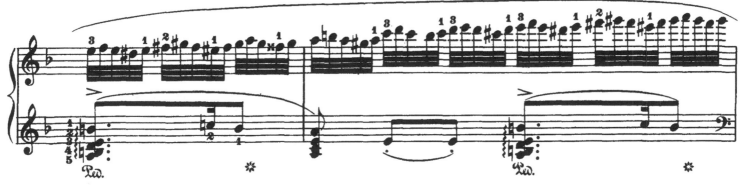

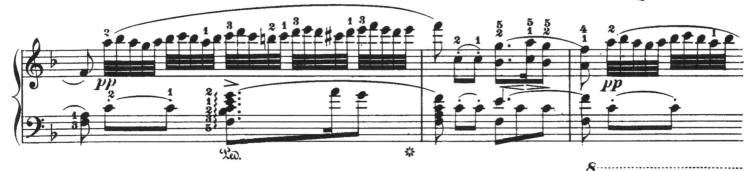

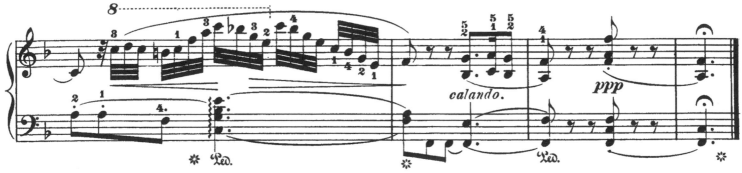

Nocturne No. 9 in E minor

John Field

Nocturne No. 4 in A Major

John Field

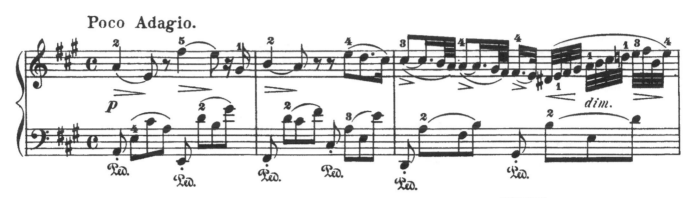

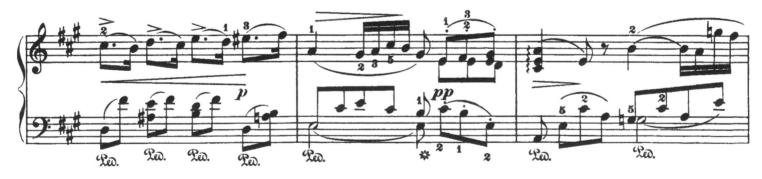

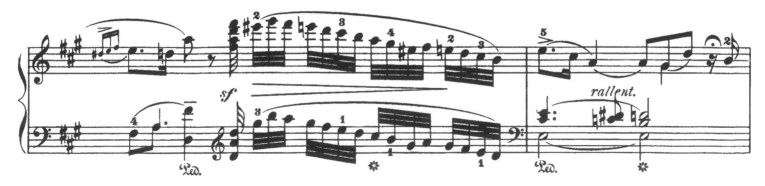

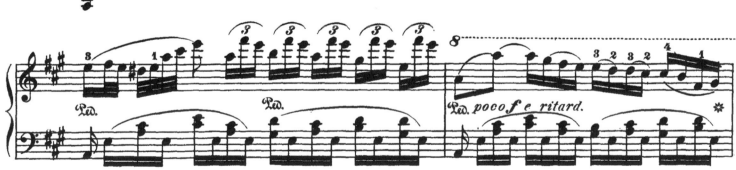